PAUL
OF TARSUS

www.realreads.co.uk

Retold by Alan Moore and Gill Tavner
Illustrated by Karen Donnelly

Published by Real Reads Ltd
Stroud, Gloucestershire, UK
www.realreads.co.uk

First published in 2010
Reprinted 2013

ISBN 978-1-906230-29-6

Printed in China by Wai Man Book Binding (China) Ltd
Designed by Lucy Guenot
Typeset by Bookcraft Ltd, Stroud, Gloucestershire

CONTENTS

THE CHARACTERS

Saul/Paul

Saul is determined to crush the 'Jesus movement'. Later, renamed Paul, he spreads the news of Jesus around the world. What happened to change him?

Simon Peter

Jesus's loyal disciple is now a leader in the growing church. Will he and Paul ever reach agreement?

Barnabas

Barnabas leads Paul to Jesus's friends. What further role will he play in Paul's work?

Ananias

Ananias lives in Damascus. What role does God want him to play in his plans for Saul?

James

James is Jesus's brother and a leader in the growing church. Can he and Paul find a way to work together?

Timothy

Timothy hears Paul preach in Lystra, and decides to help him. What will his role be?

Silas

When Silas joins Paul in Antioch, does he know that it's just the beginning of a very long journey?

PAUL OF TARSUS

This imprisonment has lasted so long, compressing my energy until the pressure feels so immense that the walls should blast apart. I need to be out there. There's so much still to do, half the world still to visit. How can I do God's work from here? I might not have much time left. I need to focus. Think, Paul, think.

People say the letters I've written during my life have been more powerful than my spoken words, but the guards won't let me send any more. Perhaps I should write an account of my life and hide it so that one day it might be found, and help people in centuries to come to understand the good news of Jesus Christ.

But can I remember all the journeys? Can I remember the people I met, the words I wrote? Will I have time? With God's grace, I will try.

My parents named me Saul. I was brought up as a Jew and as a Roman citizen in Tarsus, far from the Jewish homeland. It wasn't easy being Jewish in a Gentile society. As a minority we felt that we had to assert our identity, deliberately setting ourselves apart as God's people by strict adherence to the laws passed to us by Moses. I remember many arguments when I tried to explain to non-believers the things that made my Jewish faith so special. Perhaps adversity made us stronger, more rigid in our beliefs.

I've never been a man to do things by halves. If I believe something then I believe it with every part of my being, and I have to act upon it. I believed in the Jewish law – the Torah – and therefore I wanted to teach and enforce it. As soon as I was old enough, I travelled to Jerusalem to study to be a Pharisee.

I had a full classical education, but now I needed to concentrate on the Torah. My fervour and energy were soon noticed by the Supreme

Jewish Council – the Sanhedrin. They placed considerable authority upon my young shoulders. I loved it. I was determined that nothing should dilute or weaken the Jewish faith.

I became increasingly aware of a movement of people developing around a man called Jesus. I hadn't met Jesus, but I heard about him with concern. Although Jewish himself, Jesus was challenging our laws, sometimes openly breaking them and claiming that he had God's authority to do so. Some people said that he was the Son of God, some even claimed that he was God. This was outrageous, or so I thought at the time.

I was relieved when the Romans nailed Jesus to a wooden cross. I thought it would remove the threat he posed to Jewish unity. However, within weeks I realised that his death posed an even greater problem than his life. Stories of him rising from the dead circulated rapidly. People even claimed to have seen him. This, they said, proved that he was the Son of God, and that he had died so that our sins would be forgiven.

I refused to believe such nonsense. Not only had Jesus undermined the Torah during his lifetime, but his death by crucifixion was shameful. Jewish law teaches that anyone who dies on a tree is cursed. What would Gentiles think about Jews if we worshipped a God who allowed his own son to die in such a cursed way?

Even worse – if Jesus *was* the Son of God, we had helped the Romans to subject our God to an agonising death. We were supposed to be a light to the nations; this would make us a laughing stock.

So while Jesus's life was a problem for us, his death was a major stumbling block. The Jesus movement had to be stopped. These people wouldn't be reasoned out of their beliefs; in fact, they were prepared to die for them. While I admired this single-mindedness, indeed recognised it within myself, I had to do what was necessary. If death was the only way to stop them, they must die.

I soon gained a reputation for the brutal persecution of Jesus's followers. My name became fearful to them. My determined efforts

11

steadily enabled many synagogues to return to the uninterrupted teaching of the Torah. When I learned that Jesus's followers were preaching in the city of Damascus, I gained the Sanhedrin's permission to travel there and arrest them. I set out urgently that same day with a group of loyal men. Little could I have guessed where that road to Damascus would lead me.

At first it was a journey like any other but, as I was striding along the dusty road, a sudden blinding light, pure, brilliant white, brought me to my knees. Rather than illuminating, the light burned away my vision. Within the light I heard a voice, 'Saul, Saul, why do you persecute me?'

'Who are you?' I asked.

'I am Jesus, the man you are persecuting. Get up, go to Damascus. You will be told what to do.'

The light left me blind. My men helped me to my feet and led me into the city. For three days I was unable to eat or drink. I experienced more visions of Jesus. On the third day, I had a visitor. The man placed his trembling hands upon my shoulders. 'Brother Saul, I am Ananias. The Lord Jesus has sent me to restore your sight so that you may be filled with the Holy Spirit.'

Days earlier, I had met the risen Jesus. Now I witnessed the wonder of his power. Without a doubt, Jesus Christ was the Son of God. Ananias baptised me. At once, my sight returned and the Holy Spirit entered my heart. As I said, I've never been a man to do things by halves.

This was immense! I understood that Jesus had died and risen again so that we can start anew with God. *This* was the good news that I had to tell everyone about! That very day I began to teach that the Torah would not lead people to God. Only Jesus can do that.

The people I had come to Damascus to arrest offered me cautious hospitality – it must have been difficult to trust me. Most other Jews were furious. They had expected me to remove the threat; instead I was strengthening it. Now it was me that had to be stopped.

I travelled to Arabia. I needed to spread my message, and to learn all that I could about Jesus.

My name – Saul – troubled me. Saul, the first King of Israel, had done terrible things. Like him, I had made Saul a name to be feared. Besides, as Jesus's message wasn't only for Jews, I needed a less Jewish, more Romanised name. The name Paul means 'small' and, as I'm quite a small man, it seemed appropriate.

After an absence of nearly three years I briefly returned to Damascus. I now had a stronger message, and although

some people accepted it, many others rejected it angrily. Eventually the situation became so tense that some of my friends had to help me to escape by lowering me from the city walls in a basket.

For the first time since my conversion, I
travelled to Jerusalem. I wondered whether I would
meet the people who had known Jesus during
his lifetime. I knew they would find it difficult to
trust me. I didn't really mind whether I met them
or not – my own knowledge of Jesus was already
sufficient – but I was interested enough to allow a
man called Barnabas to lead me to them.

At first it was awkward, but they put their faith
in God. 'Stay with me,' offered Simon Peter, a man
who had been very close to Jesus. 'I have many
stories to tell you.'

Not all Jews in Jerusalem were so welcoming. As in Damascus, many were furious that I was preaching about Jesus instead of enforcing the Torah. I wasn't afraid of their fury. When I felt that I had completed my work in Jerusalem, I returned to Tarsus to prepare for the future.

Four years passed before I met Barnabas again. Having heard that I was spreading the good news about Jesus amongst both Jews and non-Jews, he came to Tarsus to seek my help. 'The Greeks in Antioch are responding well,' he explained. 'Will you come and help me?'

'Barnabas, just as you introduced me to the Jerusalem brethren, you must introduce me to the new followers in Antioch. Of course I will help you.'

Antioch now became my base. The number of believers there increased to such an extent that we gained our own identity – Christians, people called us; followers of Christ. After my first year there a famine struck Judea, causing great suffering in Jerusalem. Christians in Antioch wanted to send food to relieve the brethren in Jerusalem. Barnabas and I delivered it, then returned to Antioch.

I felt driven to teach about Jesus in as many lands as I could possibly reach. Accompanied by Barnabas and his nephew, John Mark, I sailed to Cyprus and then on to the mainland where we taught in many cities.

We met with both hostility and friendship. By the time we returned to Antioch two years later, we were confident that we had left behind us thriving communities of people prepared to live by the teachings of Jesus, who they now recognised as the Son of God.

We sailed home to a problem. Everywhere I had taught, I had spoken to Jews and non-Jews alike, for the news about Jesus is not only for Jews. Infuriatingly, in my absence, believers from Jerusalem had been telling Christians in Antioch that they must first follow the Torah in order to follow Jesus.

'The law is above all else,' they claimed. I used to say the same thing myself, but now I thought very differently. 'The law served us well until Jesus came, but we don't need it any more. Jesus is the new way forward for everybody.'

'But only if they become Jewish first,' they
insisted. This endless discussion about whether
Christ's followers should first become Jews
has dogged me ever since. I stayed in Antioch
for three more years, but the argument simply
wouldn't go away. Needing to settle it once
and for all, Barnabas and I decided to travel to
Jerusalem to discuss it with Simon Peter and the
other disciples.

Jesus's brother, James, chaired the discussion. It sometimes angers me that those who knew Jesus during his lifetime assume superiority. Like them, I have met the risen Christ. Through many visions he has taught me all I need to know. My relationship with Jesus is just as personal as theirs.

After a long and heated debate, James agreed with me. We returned to Antioch with a letter from James saying clearly that people didn't have to become Jewish in order to follow Jesus. James told me to continue preaching to Gentiles, while the Jerusalem brethren would preach to the Jews. His only other instruction was that we should continue to help the poor. With my mission clarified, I was ready to set sail again.

This time I was more ambitious. As well as revisiting the people I had already converted, I planned to travel further afield. Unfortunately, my plans were thrown at the last minute by Barnabas. He wanted to bring his nephew John Mark again, but I felt that John had let us down last time.

'Then I can't sail with you,' declared Barnabas.

I would have liked Barnabas's company, but I wouldn't compromise. Instead I took Silas, a good man who had returned with us from Jerusalem to Antioch. He would be a powerful speaker. Barnabas and I parted, and I had a new travelling companion.

At first our journey took us to places I had visited before, and I was pleased to see that communities were still strong in their belief in Jesus. In Lystra we met Timothy, who joined us in our work, and so we became three – Silas, Timothy and me – united in our determination to carry the news about Jesus to as many places as possible.

This was no easy task. We were chased from some towns, beaten in others, and in Philippi we were put in prison, but we were never afraid. In Galatia our progress stalled when I became ill, but the people welcomed us and cared for me. My illness was God's way of keeping us in Galatia long enough to carry out his work.

Later we worked among the people of Thessalonia in Greece. We didn't seek praise, because our words were God's, not our own. In order not to be a burden to the people we stayed with I earned money by working with leather and canvas. We did, however, accept donations to support the brethren in Jerusalem. We grew to love the people we met. We taught that Jesus's death allowed a new start for us all. We taught them how to deserve God's love.

We didn't try to avoid the rougher, more difficult cities. Corinth was a cosmopolitan sea port, well

known for the immoral ways of its people. Many Corinthians were preoccupied with status, judging each other by wealth and power rather than by goodness and kindness. The Holy Spirit worked through us, and in spite of the difficulties many Corinthians were baptised in Jesus's name. We were helped by Priscilla and Aquila, a very able Jewish couple who had been exiled from Rome by the Emperor Claudius. When we left Corinth, they came with us.

Whenever we left a town I felt great concern for the Christians we left behind. They faced fierce opposition and great dangers. I often wondered whether their new beliefs were strong enough. While I was busy in Athens, I sent Timothy back to Thessalonia because I was concerned about my people there. When he returned, he reassured me that they were standing firm in the Lord. I longed to visit them.

'Write them a letter,' suggested Timothy.

Grace and peace to the church of the Thessalonians from Paul, Silas and Timothy.

We thank God for you in our prayers, remembering your faith, love and hard work.

I have been worried that you might have forgotten what we taught you, but Timothy has returned to tell me that you are standing firm in God's love. I hope to visit you soon and strengthen you.

The time of Jesus's return will come suddenly, without warning, like a thief in the night. But don't worry – you won't be taken by surprise because you have heard the word of God, you live in the light. These are brutal times, but when Jesus comes he will save all of us who live and die for him, so that we will be with him forever.

Be ready. Be self-controlled. Protect yourselves with the hope of being saved by Jesus who died for us, so that we will live together with him.

I hear that you are living in a way that will please God. Continue like this. We don't need to write to you about brotherly love because we *know that you love your neighbours throughout Macedonia. Build upon this.*

Live quietly, mind your own business, work with your hands so that your work will be respected by others. Respect people who work hard and warn those who are lazy. Encourage the timid, help the weak, and be patient with everyone. Never seek revenge; be kind to all; be joyful always. Pray and give thanks. Don't discourage people or put out the spirit's fire, but listen to the truth.

May the God of peace keep you holy and may you be found blameless when the time comes.

Pray for us. The grace of Jesus Christ be with you.

Corinth was more difficult. In such a cosmopolitan city, where new ideas constantly challenged the old, it was difficult to convince people that the good news about Jesus was all they needed. After eighteen months there, although we made great progress, I left with an anxious heart.

We travelled slowly towards Jerusalem. Priscilla and Aquila agreed to stay in Ephesus where we felt they could be very effective. Eventually, Silas, Timothy and I returned to Antioch – to more trouble.

The argument about whether Christians needed to follow Jewish law was still raging. Simon Peter visited us from Jerusalem. The Torah forbids Jews from mixing with Gentiles, but we persuaded Simon Peter to ignore this and dine with us. After all, he had seen Jesus do the same.

Other Christians, brethren who were also Jews, arrived from Jerusalem, and I noticed Simon Peter withdraw from the company of Gentiles. Even Barnabas, who had led many Gentiles to Christ, withdrew from our table.

I was disappointed and angry. How many times did I have to explain that Jesus's death and resurrection changed everything? 'Jesus gave us a new start in our relationship with God,' I argued. 'The Torah isn't necessary now – all we need is faith in Jesus.'

Still Simon Peter stayed away. I had to confront him. 'Before these people came from Jerusalem you ate with Gentiles. You are a hypocrite, Simon Peter!' I could see he still thought he was right.

It wasn't only in Antioch that the brethren were making their influence felt. They were visiting lands in which I had taught about Jesus and undoing my work. I was particularly upset that they visited the Galatians, who had cared for me in my illness. 'Paul preaches falsehoods,' the visitors accused. 'He casts aside the Torah to make it easier for him to convert people. We knew the living Jesus. Paul didn't.'

The worst part of it was that the Galatians listened. They began to doubt what I had taught them.

Grace and peace to the church of the Galatians from Paul, an apostle sent by Jesus Christ.

I am astonished that you have forgotten the good news so quickly! Some people are confusing you about Jesus Christ. Their news is false. The news I teach was given to me by Jesus himself.

You know that God revealed his son to me. You know that James and Simon Peter agreed that I should preach to Gentiles. They didn't even insist that Titus, a Greek, should become Jewish before he could be a Christian.

You foolish Galatians! Who has bewitched you?
I write in a heavy hand because I am angry. You welcomed Christ, who teaches that there is no difference between Jew and Greek, between slave and free, between male and female, because we are all equal in his eyes. All that counts is faith working through love.

You received the Holy Spirit by hearing about Christ, not through the Torah. God sent his son to free us, but you are in danger of becoming slaves to the Torah. Is this what you want – to be slaves? If you become slaves to the law, Christ will be of no value to you.

The law can be summed up in one command – love your neighbour. If you insist on being slaves, be slaves in service to each other. Help each other all you can, and take pride only in your good actions. Do not allow self-indulgence and lack of self-control to get in the way of your new freedom.

May I never boast of anything except Jesus Christ. Whether you are Jew or Gentile means nothing to me. What counts is a new creation. Peace and mercy to all who follow Jesus.

I needed to follow this letter with a visit to Galatia as soon as possible. After some hurried preparations I left Antioch. Timothy and I travelled through Asia Minor. When we arrived in Galatia I found they had received my letter.

Unconvinced that it had been effective, we left to join Priscilla and Aquilla in Ephesus. Although Christians still faced great dangers there, I saw enough potential to encourage me to stay.

After many months, news reached me from Corinth that my congregations were quarrelling among themselves. It seemed that they had returned to their former concerns with status, wealth, and what they considered to be wisdom. I was deeply distressed. Such divisions would weaken them. I decided to send Timothy with a letter. He would guide them back to Christ.

Grace and peace to the church in Corinth.

I hear that you are arguing, some of you claiming to be followers of Paul, others of Peter. The truth could not be simpler – you are all followers of Christ.

Stop arguing! You don't need law courts to settle your disputes; settle them yourselves with love. Don't take pride in wealth or cleverness. For true wisdom we need the spirit of God, we must be spiritual rather than worldly-wise.

I planted a seed in Corinth, and God made it grow so you are now Christ's servants, and servants of Christ put themselves last. We must be faithful, because our eventual judgement will be by God, not by men. Christ is the head of every person, and the head of Christ is God.

I hear reports of immorality and greed. This is not Christ's way. I understand that even when you gather as a church there are divisions among you. You have misunderstood the purpose of the Lord's Supper, which is a bond between us and with Christ; it makes Christ present among us. I hear that some of you use the Lord's Supper as an opportunity to feast and get drunk, while others remain hungry.

On the night Jesus was betrayed he told his disciples to eat the bread and drink the wine in remembrance of him. It is his body and his blood. If you eat the bread or drink the cup in greed and selfishness, you sin against the body of the Lord.

Do not boast of your talents. We have all been given different spiritual gifts. They go together to make up one body, the body of Christ. All parts of the body are necessary. Use your talents to help each other and to strengthen the church. Our different gifts, whatever they may be, are nothing without love.

Love is patient and kind, not envious or boastful. Love isn't proud, rude or self-seeking. Love is not easily angered, it doesn't bear grudges. Love doesn't delight in evil; it rejoices in the truth.

It always protects, trusts, hopes and perseveres. Other gifts will pass away, but love never fails.

When I was a child I thought and talked like a child. As a man, I know many more things, but I still understand little. Only through Jesus Christ shall I reach full understanding, just as he fully understands me. When all other gifts pass away, three things remain: faith, hope, and love. The greatest of these is love.

*Christ died for our sins, was buried and raised again. He appeared to the twelve disciples, then to hundreds of his followers. Then he appeared to me. Jesus **was** raised, and this gives meaning to everything we do. Christ **has** defeated death.*

I will visit you soon. Christians here in Ephesus send you greeting.

My love to all of you in Christ Jesus.

I stayed for three years in Ephesus, but I was anxious to visit my friends in Corinth. How had my letter been received?

I was overjoyed to see my beloved
Corinthians again, but though many had
taken the words of my letter to heart, some
still questioned my authority and criticised my
preaching. One particular man insulted me,
causing me great pain. An insult to me was
an insult to all members of the churches I had
founded, so the faithful people punished him.
Realising that my presence was causing division,
I decided to leave earlier than I had planned.

Timothy and I travelled back through Macedonia. Our next significant stop was in Philippi, where news soon reached us that the Corinthians were sorry for the distress they had caused.

Greetings and comfort to the Church of God in Corinth from Paul and Timothy.

Praise God who, by comforting us in our suffering, teaches us to comfort others. We have endured great hardship and danger in our journeys. We have been beaten, imprisoned, stoned and whipped. This has taught us to rely upon God rather than upon ourselves.

We have always treated you with honesty and holiness. I am sorry that my last visit caused such pain. You have sufficiently punished the man who insulted me; now you should forgive and comfort him.

We know and trust each other, don't we? You are the result of our ministry, which is God's word, not our own. Jesus Christ opens our hearts to God's radiance. I know I am a weak person to carry such a glorious message, but my very weakness proves that the power comes from God alone, not from me.

When our earthly bodies die, we will be judged by Christ who died to free our spirit from our worldly selves. Be reconciled to God. By enduring difficulties, behaving as Christ taught and trying to be faithful, we show ourselves to be servants of God.

My beloved Corinthians, my heart is wide open to you. I would live or die for you. If I caused you sorrow by my last letter and visit, I am sorry for it, but I am happy that it led you back to God.

The Churches of Macedonia have given as much as they are able to the collection for Jerusalem. You should give generously too; your reward will be great. Your giving will not only meet the needs of God's people, but it is an expression of thanks to God.

May the grace of the Lord Jesus Christ and the love of God and the fellowship of the Holy Spirit be with you all.

I've always been a poor speaker, but what I say and do is full of the love of the Lord. When better speakers visit my congregations with different messages, they have a strong impact. This has always worried me, because they don't preach the good news of Christ's death opening our relationship with God. Instead, they usually try to lead my congregations back towards Jewish law.

It was impossible for me to be everywhere at once. As soon as I left a city, others moved into my place to undo my work. I heard that it had happened again in Corinth. As letters were now a crucial part of my ministry, I wrote another to the Corinthians.

From Paul, a true apostle of our Lord Jesus Christ, to the churches of Corinth.

Some of you say that I am timid when with you but bold in my letters, that my letters are weighty but I am a poor speaker. Remember that Christ was both meek and powerful.

Though that may be true, the words I speak have divine power to tear down, destroy and take captive any thoughts or actions levelled against Christ. We don't use the world's weapons; we use gentle weapons to do our work. I am not ashamed to boast of the authority God gave to me. We brought you the good news, and we hope to spread it further.

I don't want my letters to frighten you, but I'm afraid that you will be led astray by better preachers who preach a different Jesus than the one we know. They boast of their abilities, and take from you. Why do you put up with them?

I love you, and Christ, more than they do. I take nothing from you. I have suffered flogging, imprisonment, shipwrecks and dangers, and daily I *live with concern for my churches. If you're weak, I feel weak. If you sin, I burn inwardly. I boast of the things that show my weakness because they also show Christ's strength and love. I have often pleaded with God to take away my physical weakness, but he replied, 'My love is enough; my power is made perfect in weakness.'*

I want to visit you again. I don't want your possessions, I want you. I will gladly give all that I have and all that I am for you.

Will I still find you arguing? During my last visit I warned that I would punish those who continue to sin, because Christ speaks through me and he is not weak in dealing with you. I write strongly so that I won't have to make harsh use of God's authority when I am with you.

The God of love and peace be with you.

Through God's grace, the people of Corinth returned to Christ. There were now flourishing Christian communities all the way from Jerusalem around the inland sea and throughout Macedonia.

I decided to embark on a journey I had often longed to make. I wanted to preach about Jesus in Spain – and beyond. I would travel via Rome, the capital of the Roman Empire. There were already strong Christian communities in Rome – the news had spread there by others doing God's work – but they were heavily persecuted and needed encouragement.

Before I could set sail, I had to deliver the collection from Corinth to the churches in Jerusalem. I wrote to the Roman church about my plans.

Grace and peace to God's people in Rome.

I pray that I can visit you soon. God will reward with eternal life people who continue to do good. He will be angry with those who do evil. Jesus's death and resurrection reveal God's faith from the beginning to the end. Having heard the good news, you have no excuse for wickedness.

Do not judge others. Only God can judge. He will judge each of us, whether Jew or Gentile, because he loves us equally. The Torah is not important; we can sin and perish with or without the law. The real value in being a Jew is the knowledge that Jews were entrusted with the word of God. Righteousness through faith in Christ is there for all who believe.

As Christians we endure great suffering, but this develops our perseverance, character and hope. Our present suffering is nothing compared with the glory to come.

Through Jesus's death we have died to the power of sin; it has no power over us because we are alive to God in Jesus Christ. Offer yourselves in service, as living sacrifices to God. This will lead to holiness and eternal life, whereas sin leads to death. The Torah is not sin, but it preoccupies us with sin whilst Christ Jesus calls us to be concerned with goodness. None of us is perfect because even our best efforts go wrong, but if the Holy Spirit works in us our spirit is alive with goodness.

God works for the good of those who love him. Nothing can separate us from the love of God that is in Christ Jesus. If you proclaim that Jesus is Lord and believe in your heart that God raised him from the dead, you will be saved.

Use your gifts to help each other, not to impress the world. Be sincere. Hate evil and cling to good. Honour others above yourselves. Be joyful in hope, patient in suffering, faithful in prayer. Share with those in need, and offer hospitality. Rejoice with those who rejoice; mourn with those who mourn. Bless those who persecute you, and feed your enemy if he is hungry. Overcome evil with good. Work towards peace.

Love your neighbour as yourself, and stop passing judgement on each other. The strong among you must bear with the failings of the weak; you must accept one another just as Christ accepts you.

I am convinced that you are full of goodness. I will visit you on my way to Spain, but first I must go to Jerusalem, even though I have been warned against it. Pray for me. Glory to God forever.

Unfortunately things didn't go according to plan – God's plans were quite different. It was to be three long years before I finally arrived in Rome, and then as a prisoner.

From Corinth I took the collection to Jerusalem, where it came as no surprise to find myself at the centre of a riot when I visited the temple. Fortunately I am a Roman citizen as well as a Jew and a Christian, so Roman soldiers saved me from the bloodthirsty crowd by arresting me.

My friends and I, including Timothy, were taken to Caesarea, where the Romans kept us for two years before deciding to take us to Rome. At last we were going to Rome, even if it wasn't in the way we had intended. But God had yet another surprise for me.

It was early autumn, a dangerous time of year to sail on the Mediterranean. In a violent

storm we were shipwrecked on the shore of
Malta. By God's grace, everybody from the ship
survived. God had given me this unexpected
opportunity to introduce the good news about
Jesus to Malta. It was three months before we
had a ship to continue our journey. Eventually
we reached mainland Italy, and walked the rest
of the way to Rome.

My imprisonment until now has been light. I have been allowed to receive visitors and even to talk to people about Jesus. It is only recently, since I was formally charged, that they have stopped these favours and stopped me sending letters. Before that, I managed to write to the church in Philippi.

From Paul and Timothy to all Christ's saints in Philippi.

My shipwreck in Malta and imprisonment in Rome have helped to advance the good news. My guards see how I bear my chains for Christ, and Christians in Rome now speak more fearlessly. I rejoice because I know that through your prayers and the spirit of Jesus Christ I will be delivered – somehow. I don't know whether I am to live or to die. It would be better to die and to be with Christ, but as it is more important to continue my work, I trust they will spare me.

Don't be frightened of those who oppose you. Your courage will show them that they will be destroyed and you will be saved by Christ. Christ gives us encouragement, comfort and compassion. Like him, we should be servants to others and do everything with humility. In this dark world you will shine like stars.

I want to know Christ and to share in his suffering so that I too may have eternal life. I am imperfect, but God has called me. The destiny of Christ's enemies is destruction, but we await the Lord who will save us. Stand firm. Concentrate on all that is true, noble, pure and admirable. The peace of God which is beyond all understanding will guard your hearts and minds.

Thank you for your concern for me. Don't worry — I have strength for anything through Jesus Christ. You have sent generous gifts which I welcome; they are pleasing to God, and he will reward you with his glorious riches in Christ Jesus.

I hope to send Timothy to you soon. I will follow.

The grace of our Lord Jesus Christ be with you.

That was one of the last letters I sent. My situation is now serious by the ways of the world, but I'm not afraid of death. I have my faith to strengthen me. I constantly rejoice in my blessings from the Lord.

They have charged me with challenging Roman authority by preaching that Christ is the one true Lord, but as I have taught people to respect Roman authority they won't be able to prove this case against me.

The second charge, however, is more justified. I refuse to worship the Emperor as a god because there is only one true God. Should it be my fate to die, I look forward to meeting Christ in person, but I believe that I will be freed. I am sure God has more work for me to do.

I thank God that I have had time to complete this account. May you who read it live in the love of Jesus Christ.

MACEDONIA

Rome

ITALY

Philippi

Thessalonica

THESSAL

SPAIN

GREECE

Corinth

MALTA

MEDITERRANEAN

PAUL'S TRAVELS

0   100   200   300   400   500 miles

N
W   E
S

BLACK SEA

GALATIA

IA

ASIA MINOR

Ephesus   Lystra

Tarsus
Antioch

SYRIA

CYPRUS

Damascus

SEA

Caesarea Philippi

PALESTINE

Jerusalem
JUDEA

ARABIA

TAKING THINGS FURTHER
The real read

This *Real Reads* volume of *Paul of Tarsus* is our interpretation of some of the events of the New Testament, told from the perspective of one of its most influential participants. In writing this account of Paul's life, we have used evidence from both The Acts of the Apostles and from some of Paul's letters, known as epistles, found in later books of the New Testament.

It is important to acknowledge that Acts of the Apostles and Paul's epistles are often contradictory. When difficulties arose, we tried to use evidence from the epistles rather than from Acts, as they are Paul's actual words. There is, however, uncertainty about which epistles were genuinely written by Paul. We have used those most commonly accepted as 'Pauline' epistles – Romans 1 and 2, Corinthians, Galatians, Philippians and Thessalonians 1. Philemon is also recognised as Paul's work, but was not necessary for our story.

At first, inconsistencies made our task rather difficult, until we realised that what we needed to do was present the New Testament as it is, rather than weave a path of our choice. Therefore, if you read *Real Reads Simon Peter*, for which we used Acts as a source, and *Real Reads Paul of Tarsus*, you may well notice some of the apparent contradictions and inconsistencies that are present in the Bible itself.

Although Paul's own writings provide us with a wealth of evidence to draw upon, we have also had to fill in some gaps by trying to imagine what he might have been like and what he might have thought. We have always based our work on thorough research and close attention to the Bible account.

This *Real Reads Paul of Tarsus* does not cover all the events of the New Testament. Reading the other five books in the series will bring you closer to an understanding of the complete story. You may then want to read the New Testament itself. We recommend that you read either the *New International Version* or *The Youth Bible*, details of which are given below.

Biblical sources

On the *Real Reads* website you will find an
online concordance (www.realreads.co.uk/
newtestament/concordance/paul). A 'bible
concordance' is an indexing tool which allows
you to see how the same words, sentences
and passages appear in different versions
and translations of the Bible. This online
concordance will direct you from events in the
Real Reads version back to their biblical sources,
so you can see clearly where each part of our
story is drawn from.

Life in
New Testament times

Paul was brought up as a Jew in Tarsus, in what
is now southern Turkey. Tarsus is a long way
from Palestine, so influences upon the young
Paul would have been quite different from the
childhood experiences of Jesus and his friends.
Jews in Tarsus were a minority, meaning that
Paul lived among Gentiles. He would probably

have spoken at least two languages and, as Tarsus was known as an intellectual centre, he could have received a thorough classical education.

Tarsus, like Judea, was within the Roman Empire. At the time, the Romans ruled most of the land bordering the Mediterranean. In order to move around their enormous empire, the Romans built an impressive transport network, which helped to make Paul's travels much easier than they would otherwise have been. Over a period of thirty years, Paul travelled about ten thousand miles.

Paul visited many of the major cities of the time. Although these would have looked impressive, many of their inhabitants lived in great poverty. These people needed something to give them hope and purpose. The word 'gospel' means good news – Paul brought them good news about how they could live, and taught that Jesus's death gave everybody the chance of eternal happiness after a life of goodness. Paul believed that this message was for everybody, not only for Jews.

Within the Roman Empire people worshipped many different gods. Paul's message – as had been the message of all Jews for the past two thousand years – was that there was only one true god.

Unfortunately for Paul, many Jews saw all teaching about Jesus as a threat to their own religion. Romans too saw the new Christian movement as a problem – not least because they insisted that the Emperor was a god. As a result, Christians were heavily persecuted by both Jews and Romans. The beginnings of the early church were therefore far from easy or peaceful. The early Christians were courageous people, so convinced of the truth of Jesus that they were prepared to die for it. Paul himself suffered many severe beatings and imprisonment, and it is commonly believed that he eventually died for his Christian beliefs.

Paul's life and teaching have shaped Christianity into the faith it is today. By preaching to Gentiles he transformed what was a small Jewish sect into the beginnings of a world religion which would long outlast the Roman Empire.

Finding out more

We recommend the following books and websites to gain a greater understanding of Paul and his role in the New Testament.

Books

We strongly recommend that you read the rest of the *Real Reads* New Testament series, as the six narratives interlock to give a more complete picture of events. These are *Jesus of Nazareth, Mary of Galilee, Simon Peter, Judas Iscariot* and *Mary Magdalene.*

● *New Century Youth Bible*, Authentic Lifestyle, 2007.

● *Paul's Travels*, Tim Dowley, Candle Books, 2009.

● *Paul: A Novel*, Walter Wangerin, Lion Hudson, 2001.

● *In the Steps of Saint Paul: An Illustrated Guide to Paul's Journeys*, Peter Walker, Lion Hudson, 2008.

Websites

● www.apostlepaulthefilm.com/paul
Includes an interactive timeline in which Paul's life is shown alongside historical events, and animated maps of his journeys.

● www.gardenofpraise.com/bibleles.htm#paul
Lots of information, ideas and activities.

● www.ccel.org/bible/phillips/
CN600NTWORLD.htm
Short articles about the Roman Empire in New Testament times, accompanied by maps.

TV and film

● *Saul of Tarsus* and *The Ministry of Paul*, two titles from *Animated Stories from the New Testament*, directed by Richard Rich, Boulevard Entertainment, 1990.

● *Apostle Paul and the Earliest Churches*, Vision Video, 2005. A 50-minute documentary about Paul's ministry in what is now Turkey.